Weather in Fall

BY JENNA LEE GLEISNER

The
**Child's
World®**
childsworld.com

Published by The Child's World®
1980 Lookout Drive • Mankato, MN 56003-1705
800-599-READ • www.childsworld.com

Photographs ©: iStockphoto, cover, 9, 10; Andrew
Mayovskyy/Shutterstock Images, 4–5; George W. Bailey/
Shutterstock Images, 6; Shutterstock Images, 12–13,
14, 20–21; iStockphoto/Thinkstock, 17; Serr Novik/
iStockphoto, 19

Design Element: Shutterstock Images

ISBN 9781503816657
LCCN 2016945901

Printed in the United States of America
PA02323

ABOUT THE AUTHOR

Jenna Lee Gleisner is an author
and editor from Minnesota.
Her favorite thing about fall is
the changing colors and cooler
weather.

Contents

CHAPTER 1

Cool Weather ...4

CHAPTER 2

Fall Changes ...12

CHAPTER 3

Warmer Clothes ...18

Wind Spinner Craft...22
Glossary...23
To Learn More...24
Index...24

Cool Weather

It is a fall morning.

It is **chilly**.

Fall weather is often cloudy and windy.

Fall comes after
the warm summer.
Temperatures drop.

9

It gets cold enough for **frost**. Frost forms on grass.

Fall Changes

Cool weather changes plants. They stop growing.

Leaves fall from trees.
Wind blows the leaves
around.

Animals feel it get colder.

Some grow more **fur**.

Warmer Clothes

People feel it get colder in fall, too. They wear jackets. They wear hats and mittens.

Fall weather gets colder and colder. Soon winter will be here!

Wind Spinner Craft

Make your own wind spinner!

Supplies:

paper plate   scissors
pencil   string
markers

Instructions:

1. Start at the outer edge of the paper plate. With your pencil, draw a spiral inward toward the middle.

2. Draw your favorite objects on the plate with markers.

3. Use your scissors to cut along the penciled line.

4. Poke a small hole in the center of the plate.

5. Pull the string through the hole. Tie a knot in the end.

6. Hang your spinner outside. Then watch it spin in the wind!

Glossary

chilly — (CHIL-ee) Chilly means cold. Fall is chilly.

frost — (FRAWST) Frost is a thin layer of ice. Frost forms in fall when temperatures go below freezing.

fur — (FUR) Fur is the hair on an animal. Some animals grow thicker fur in fall.

To Learn More

Books

Appleby, Alex. *What Happens in Fall?* New York, NY: Gareth Stevens Publishing, 2014.

Felix, Rebecca. *How's the Weather in Fall?* Ann Arbor, MI: Cherry Lake Publishing, 2013.

Web Sites

Visit our Web site for links about fall weather: **childsworld.com/links**

Note to Parents, Teachers, and Librarians: We routinely verify our Web links to make sure they are safe and active sites. So encourage your readers to check them out!

Index

cloudy, 7
cold, 11, 16, 18, 20

frost, 11

jackets, 18

summer, 8

windy, 7
winter, 20